The Great American Credit Secret

The Great American Credit Secret

Antoine Sallis

Published by Game Changer Publishing

ISBN Paperback: 979-8-9863238-1-7
ISBN Digital: 979-8-9863238-0-0
ISBN Hardcover: 978-1-961189-27-0

Game Changer PUBLISHING

www.PublishABestSellingBook.com

DEDICATION

This book is dedicated to my son, Antoine Sallis II. Unlocking the Secrets of the world will yield you the life of your dreams.

FREE GIFTS

DOWNLOAD YOUR FREE GIFTS

Read This First

Just to say thanks for buying and reading my book, I would like to give you a few free bonus gifts, no strings attached!

To Download Now, Visit:

Foreword

Your credit is your life report card. But the truth is many people don't understand it. They do not like to talk about it and that's why so many fail. I made it my mission to help educate as many people about credit as possible.

I have motivated and encouraged millions of people to improve their financial literacy. This is a way for me to give back. I began looking for like-minded people who want to empower others through financial education and I found Carlos D Smith. Together we began teaching others about the power of credit. Carlos introduced me to Antoine and his philosophy, 'The Great American Credit Secret'. Instantly I saw the potential of helping even more people through his unique program. It's no secret that we need credit for the most important things in life. The secret is how we go about doing it to achieve the ultimate benefits. We all have dreams and goals - we just have to know how to get it. This book gives you the blueprint.

When Antoine asked, "why don't they teach this in school?" I have also asked myself the same question over the years. When I read the book, I knew instantly that this book has life changing inside information that everyone will benefit from. Be ready to live the life of your dreams because there is NO LIMIT to your success through the financial education you will receive by reading The Great American Credit Secret.

Percy "Master P" Miller

Entrepreneurial Businessman, Philanthropist and Music Mogul

The Great American Credit Secret

Antoine Sallis

Game Changer PUBLISHING

www.PublishABestSellingBook.com

Table of Contents

CHAPTER 1

The Great American Credit Secret

We have all been lied to. For years. Let me explain...

Have you ever wondered why they don't teach credit in school? They tell us to get a good job. They tell us to get a good career. They tell us to lead this amazing life, delve deep into our studies, and go to college. But they do not tell us about credit.

Schools teach that buying a home is the American dream. It's literally known as the American dream—buying a home, and working a good job in the United States of America. But not once do they mention that you need a good credit score to buy your home. Why is this?

Let's think about student loans. When kids go to college, the first thing they do at the admissions office is sign you up for student loans to pay for your college tuition. Some of these student loans are massive amounts. I've seen student loans up to a million dollars depending on the curriculum and how deep a student is going with their academic studies. But looking at the credit report, why is there nowhere on the school's curriculum that explains what a million dollars in student loan debt does? What does a million dollars in student loan debt mean to the average person? These are questions that many people do not know the answer to. These are questions that the folks in the school's administration office have not answered. These are questions that are not explained to us in school. Why is this? There has to be a reason. It cannot be a coincidence.

Banks do not like credit repair companies. How do we know? One reason is that if a credit repair company opens up an account, it gets shut down most of the time. Another reason we know that banks do not like credit repair companies is that a bank will not give a credit repair company a merchant account. They see it as a conflict of interest. So, in essence, a bank feels competition with a company helping clients fix and repair their credit profile. Go figure!

The United States of America is the most powerful country in the world. One of the things America prides itself on is the educational system. If this is so, how are we missing such a huge component of our lives by not teaching credit in school? Have you ever wondered that? Credit is one of the biggest factors in the U.S. In fact, statistics show credit is 75% of every buying decision that you make. So with that being said, the fact that they don't teach us this in school, the fact that they don't pound this into our brains, what does that mean? Is it an accident? Did they accidentally forget to tell us about the most important thing in our lives? The truth is no. It's not an accident.

The truth is that credit is meant to naturally and organically be utilized so that the bureaus can dictate what your spending patterns are and what your payback patterns are. It's risk assessment that is assessed. Do you naturally pay your bills on time? Do you naturally open up different types of accounts? They do not want you to strategically place your credit and build your credit to a certain aspect to get approved for things in life that will give you low interest rates, high credit limits, and high revolving amounts. They want that to be a natural thing. They do not want you to know how to formulate your credit profile on your own. *This* is why they do not want credit taught in schools. *This* is why it's a secret.

The average consumer does not truly realize or understand the depth, the gravity, and the power of credit. If they did, then with the same energy, the same determination, and the same passion that students use to earn a degree, and the same passion that compels the average human being to spend hundreds of thousands of dollars on their education, they would utilize that same energy for building the most powerful credit score ever (And it wouldn't even take 10% of that effort). There's only a very, very small sliver of Americans chasing credit like their lives depend on it because they understand how powerful credit truly is. These individuals who do understand are a small percentage of the country's population. These individuals truly know and understand *The Great American Credit Secret.*

Here's an example: Let's say I'm going to school with one of my best friends, and then his parents add him to their credit card as an Authorized User. His parents' credit card will show up on his credit report. So if they've had a good payment history and had on-time payments and a big credit limit, that will show up on my friend's credit report. So then suppose I say to my friend, "Hey, let's go get a cell phone," and we go to the Verizon store. We're the same age. We've been buddies for years. We both want the newest iPhone. The Verizon salesperson tells my friend, "Well, sir, you are approved for the iPhone and you only have to pay the taxes on it, which is only $130."

I see my friend with his new cell phone, and I say, "Wow, this is great, this is great! Yes! Sign me up as well."

However, when they run my credit to sign me up, they see there's nothing on the credit file. And since there's nothing on a credit file, Verizon says, "Yes, you are approved, but… you just have to put down 50% of the phone's value."

And I say, "Oh, what does that mean?"

"Well, the phone is $1,300, so you have to pay $675."

I look at my friend, but now I'm 100% confused. In my mind, I'm thinking, *What just happened here? Why do I have to pay more than him? Why didn't I qualify with the minimum down like my friend?*

This is an everyday scenario. It comes from ignorance of not truly knowing and understanding the power of credit. The sad part about this illustration is that it is only a small example of why having good credit is important. On a larger scale, people with bad credit pay up to millions of dollars more over a lifetime than someone with good credit pays. It's kind of ironic if you truly think about the system. *Some may say that it has a glitch.*

If someone has good credit, the typical person would think that they have the money to afford their bills, so why should someone who does not have money to pay their bills and has bad credit, why should they pay more? Well, ironically, that essentially is exactly what is happening. Many would argue that if someone has bad credit, it's a bigger risk for the lender, so they have to charge higher interest—I beg to differ. Those higher interest rates keep many banks in business, and if those with bad credit are being charged higher interest rates, it essentially makes them have to dig a deeper hole in the credit world.

Credit has so many components. This book is geared towards helping you understand what they are. Lenders, banks, the credit bureaus and collection agencies DO NOT want you to read this book! They do not want you to understand what is *really* going on with your credit. But this is America! The land of free speech, so I will tell you what you need to know!

I'm going to share with you ***The Great American Credit Secret.***

Credit can change your life. Even someone who grew up in poverty can take advantage and structure their credit score so that in *six to eight months,* they will have a line of credit for $50,000 to $100,000. This may be someone who's grown up in poverty and does not have rich friends or parents with a nest egg saved up. For them to build it up only takes a minimal amount of money and some strategy. Yet credit is something that continuously multiplies. What a phenomenon! Someone who grew up in poverty with little to no money can take a credit score (regardless of credit history, bad credit, or good credit) and multiply it to $50k-$100k in six months and then multiply that to half a million within 18 months with the right strategy.

Here's an example: Let's say you get financed for a car on your credit report and let's say it's your first car, so it's only $8,000. You saved enough money for the 20% down payment, $1,600, and financed the rest, give or take $6,400.

Now you have a $6,400 line of credit on your credit report as an auto. When I say credit multiplies, that means that once you make 60% of the monthly payments on time over six months, you can go back to the dealership, and they immediately would give you another car up to double that value with little to no down payment.

Now, suppose you were to go to two dealerships. One dealership approves you for up to double that first car value. Then you go to another dealership, and they will do the exact same thing. That's why many people get into the car rental industry because they found a way to get multiple cars on their credit reports. If you apply for four to five cars within a two-week window, you will get approved. This is important because no bank will approve you once a new car shows up on your credit report unless you make over $300k per year. With this tactic, you just got five cars! You can also get vehicles to report to your business. This is also a secret that many do not want you to know and understand. This is exactly what I mean when I say that credit multiplies. However, if you own a business there are many advantages to getting additional vehicles under your business. Just keep this one rule in mind: in most situations before you get a vehicle in your business name you should ALWAYS have a vehicle on your personal credit profile.

The same rule of multiplication exists for a credit card. Let's say you have a card with a $2,000 limit. If you paid that credit card on time for six months to a year, you can go back to another bank and ask for another card, and they're going to want to give you double, if not more of the limit of that first card. So imagine if you go to multiple banks, now you have multiple credit cards. Again, that's what we mean when we say credit multiplies. Again, it's the exact same theory with business credit, but even more substantial.

That is something that people do not understand, especially in this age of entrepreneurship, where people want to start and own their own businesses. It's more important than ever to understand this power of credit because the number one reason businesses fail in the first two years is lack of funding. Well, what is funding? Funding is the ability to have capital, working capital, for your business. For someone who doesn't have someone to give them a big loan to start their business, they will look at one thing.

That thing is credit.

If you truly understand credit and the positive impact it can have on your life, you will fight for it as if you couldn't breathe without it. You will learn it inside and out, every aspect that you could possibly find. You will research and look it up and understand what it means. The people who truly understand the power of credit do not ever use their debit card. *This is a secret.* A lot of people know it, but most people don't. People who truly understand the power of credit only use their credit cards.

Here is the explanation of why. If you use your debit card to buy a computer for $1,000, you have $1,000 going out of your bank account—no big deal. If you use your credit card to make that same purchase for $1,000, almost every credit card out there offers incentives such as points (points equate to travel credits, points equate to hotel stays, and points equate to cashback). So someone else uses their credit card to buy the exact same $1,000 computer, they're gaining points. And guess what else? They're putting usage on their credit card. Once they use that credit card, they pay it down. That triggers algorithms in the bank because they track your spending habits, prompting the bank to increase your limit. When they increase your credit limit, your credit score increases!

Have you ever received a call from the bank or an email asking you to update your income? They're trying to determine if you are ready for a credit line increase. *This is a secret.* They want to give you more credit, which boosts your credit score. Why is this? Because the banks work off of interest. Every time you use those credit cards and carry a small balance, you pay interest. That's how the banks make their money. But paying that small amount of interest is nothing compared to the points you will gain or other benefits from using your credit card.

I know people who travel the world for free at least once a year by making regular purchases on their credit cards. That's a free vacation. And then what happens to your credit profile itself? Well, one of the things about credit is that it's based on credit, how much available credit is on your credit report. So if you're getting credit limits on your credit card increased, that naturally increases your credit score. The number of points it goes up is contingent on how much they give you.

I've seen a credit card limit increase from $11,000 to $25,000. The client got maybe 60 points of an increase on their credit score by naturally behaving in an educated way while using their credit.

I advise you to take your time and energy to read and reread this book as many times as possible. We are giving you jewels and gifts that, if applied, will completely change your life.

We are teaching you things that very few know. What we are teaching you is *The Great American Credit Secret.*

Notes

Notes

Notes

Notes

Notes

Notes

Notes

Notes

Notes

Notes

Notes

Notes

Notes

CHAPTER 2

Buying Power Secrets

What is buying power? Why is it so important?

Well, that's what we're here to discuss. Buying power regarding your credit report means what items you can afford, how much of an item you can afford, and how much a bank is willing to fund you based on what they see on your credit report. That is buying power.

Buying power is not something that a lot of people know about. It's not something that's talked a lot about. Only every now and then, when you finally progress and move up to make a big purchase in life, if you don't qualify, unfortunately, is when most people find out what it is because the lender now has to explain to you why you do not qualify. I'm going to illustrate a few things throughout this chapter in relation to buying power.

The first and biggest one that comes to mind is "The American Dream," which is owning a home in the United States. Home buying power in relation to owning a home means essentially how much of a house can you buy? How big of a house can you buy? How expensive of a house can you afford? And can you afford the monthly payments that are associated with that house? Several things will dictate this.

When it comes to getting a mortgage, they will ask you three main things. Think of buying a home as a three-legged stool: One leg is credit, one leg is proof of income (how much you make per year), and the third leg is down payment.

When it comes to buying a home, those three things dictate your buying power.

If you want a million-dollar home in California, they need to look at those three factors. The beautiful part is that when it comes to credit, your credit report in association with the mortgage does not dictate your buying power as much as the other two factors. This means that when it comes to having a mortgage on your credit report, the main thing they are looking at is the age of your credit report.

So when it comes to buying a home, remember the three-legged stool: down payment, proof of income, and credit.

When it comes to buying a home, the down payment is a big part of how much of a home you can afford. Beware of people who say you can get a low down payment as a first-time homebuyer. That is true, but at what cost? Standing in line for the first-time buyer's program can be like standing in line at a welfare office.

The more of a down payment you have, the better. Down payments range from 2% to 10%, depending on what type of mortgage you're getting. Is it an FHA? Is it conventional? Is it an investment property?

People who have a big down payment are the first ones to qualify for a home. If you're a first-time homebuyer and I'm a first-time homebuyer, and you and I are looking at the same home, but you have a huge down payment ready, then you're going to get the home. I have to essentially stand around and wait until there's an available home where no one is bidding to get into the first-time buyer's program. It is not a situation where people are eager to help you get a home with no money down. The people who have money to put down will always be chosen first. So if you have no choice in the matter and have to buy a home, you can look into going with the first-time homebuyer's program. But I would use that as a last alternative. I would do everything in my power to come up with the down payment for buying that home because having a mortgage is like having money in the bank. Most properties earn equity. Rarely does your property not earn or gain equity.

The second portion of that three-legged stool we spoke about is proof of income. The more money you make, the better.

Here's another secret... If you have multiple people living in your household, a wife or even a brother or sister living with you, you can include their income. Including their income will help you qualify for a larger house.

Be diligent, however, in including income because when you include their income, you also have to include their credit score. If they have a great credit score, then it works out. But if they have a lower credit score, it will work against you.

Here's another little-known secret when adding people to include or increase your income. You can add someone to the loan but not the title, meaning that you can have them added to the loan so they can help you get approved for the home, but you do not have to add them to the title. So if you're the one primarily putting up all the cash and you're the one paying the house note, then it's your house. You'll be on the title. They will not have access to or ownership of it.

Ok, back to the second leg of the stool: Proof of income. The more income you can produce or provide, the better. That's why it's important to have a good tax guy, a good accountant (CPA).

Sometimes we make money on the side with little side gigs, and we don't report it because we want to save a few bucks from Uncle Sam. Traditionally, this is not something the government will look kindly upon because every American citizen has to pay all their taxes. However, keep in mind that if you're making side income and you do file it, then that's the extra income you can include when buying your home. So that's another way that you can get more house.

The last leg of that three-legged stool is credit. When it comes to buying a home, the good news is that most people think you have to have some phenomenally high credit score. This is not the case at all.

There are only essentially three credit brackets depending on which state you are in, but the highest bracket is a 760 score. You could qualify for a home with a 640 credit score in some states. I would encourage you to continue to get your credit as high as possible, but when applying for a mortgage with credit, lenders are only looking at the number and the DTI, which is your Debt to Income ratio. Meaning that if you have negative accounts, collections, or repossessions on there for a high amount of money, that will throw off your DTI even if you have a good credit score. That's why it's important to make sure that your credit is clear before applying for a mortgage or buying a home.

Here's another secret... If you have a bunch of collections on your credit report and they are small bills, it will not stop you from getting a home, especially if you make a large amount of income. Some people say "I want to wait until I have perfect credit to buy a house." Why? To avoid a slightly higher APR perhaps? You may want to think again. You will pay more in rent (which is essentially paying someone else's mortgage) because you don't want a potentially higher APR that could be $200 more a month? That makes no sense. Plus, if you get the home asap then as soon as your score gets higher you can refinance and get that better rate. That's the smart way.

I've seen people with a great job, with 14 medical bills in collections on their credit report, who still have a 720 credit score and get approved for the home of their dreams. Should you try to get those removed before applying for the home? Absolutely.

But if you are on a certain timetable and you have to get your home, do not let that stop you. Why is this? Because a mortgage is the biggest and most powerful tradeline you can have on your credit report. The only penalty you will face from the previous situation we just explained is that you will not get the best APR (Annual Percentage Rate), and that's okay. APR is higher for people with the worst credit, meaning that your mortgage will be higher. This is not a good thing, but guess what? After you start building your credit, making on-time mortgage payments, and getting rid of those negative collections, you can refinance your home and get a better interest rate. That would be a great refinancing strategy.

So remember, concerning credit and getting a mortgage, lenders care most about your debt to income ratio and the score itself. That's the beautiful thing. As long as you have mastered those two things on your credit report, you will get approved for your home. And again, I can't stress this enough, having a mortgage on your credit report is the most powerful thing any individual could have on their credit report.

That completes the mortgage section, which is one form of buying power.

Here's another example of buying power: Banks give out personal loans, and banks give out credit cards.

When the bank is deciding whether they're going to give you a loan or not, they are mostly looking at installments on your credit report. What is an installment? An installment is an item with a fixed amount, meaning that once you pay it, it's done. Some examples of installments are vehicles, a house, or a loan. A student loan is also an example of an installment; once you pay it off, it's done. However a student loan doesn't give you the same amount of buying power that a personal loan, auto or mortgage will have.

A credit card is a revolving account; you pay it, but it's still not done. You can still keep going back and using it. That's a revolving account. Banks, however, look at your installment accounts when deciding whether to give you a loan and how much of a loan to give you. *That's a secret.*

Let's take a look at an example: If you have a $400,000 house and you've paid on time for the last four years, they know that's a big installment and that they can loan you some money. If they've seen you've paid off three or four vehicles over the past few years, then they know there have not been missed payments. These are the key factors they are looking at when deciding whether you will be approved for the loan.

So the next question becomes, how much? Several factors answer that question. Let's look at a few of them:

1. How much were the installments that were on the credit report before? Was it a $100,000 house, or was it a $500,000 house? Was the car you paid off an $8,000 car, or was it a $50,000 car? The higher the item you've paid on or paid off, the bigger the loan they will give you. Keep in mind that the item does not have to be fully paid off for the banks to give you a loan. They just have to see a consistent record of being paid on time.

2. The second question to decide your limit is how much income you make? Income plays a huge factor. Lenders and banks look at your income on a signature loan. Most banks will loan you up to 50% of your proof of income. For example, if someone makes $120,000 a year, most banks are willing to give them up to a $60,000 loan because it's 50% of their income. Keep in mind that banks have different limits on signature loans. Some banks only give out $35,000, while others give out up to $100,000. Most banks only go up to $50,000. Some lending companies give up to $100,000.

Lending companies are similar to banks because their sole purpose is to give out loans. They would not be in business if they did not give out loans. They profit off of the interest from the loans. So if you think about it, if a bank does not give out loans, if a lending company does not lend, then there is no lending company.

This philosophy is very important to understand because many people walk into the bank with a fear that they won't be qualified. In reality, the banks are the ones that need your business. Without us, they would not exist. Could you imagine if a lending company did not lend to any clients? They would have nothing. So your job is to walk into that bank looking as good as you can by having your buying power in order.

Now that you know to have your buying power ready and have your proof of income ready, you can go in and get funded for your signature loan or whatever you need.

Speaking of funding, when filling out applications, remember that banks are looking for stability. Is it stability if you move from house to house or job to job? If you are using a P.O. Box, you are more of a risk than someone who's been in their home for 12 years. This same rule applies to employment. If you have been at your job for 15 years, this is less of a risk than someone going from job to job in the last nine months.

Also, what gives banks assurance is knowing that you make a good amount of money compared to someone whose annual income is only $25k per year.

Rent is also important because it's a huge factor in your debt to income. If you pay $1,000 a month in rent but only make $35,000 per year, you are only left with $23,000. Therefore, you cannot expect a bank or lender to approve you for a large amount of money.

This is the philosophy of buying power. This is why buying power is important. To simplify it, buying power is the culmination of the type of tradeline you have on your credit report and the amount of your income. Remember, a tradeline is anything that reports to your credit. So the value, the amount of money on that tradeline, how much money you make at your regular job or if you own a business, how much money you make in your business, and how long you've been paying on these items determines your buying power. Banks use that to decide how much money to give you and in what increments.

This is something that you can structure and strategize yourself. There are different ways and tools to do this for someone with absolutely no credit and is new to the game. You can go to a company called Self Lender. Once you sign up for Selflender.com and pay $30 a month, they will give you a tradeline for around $1,500. This is a Certificate of Deposit that reports to your credit profile like an installment loan. Every month you pay into it, it is recorded on your credit report. At the end of the year, you get a majority of the funds back. On Self Lender, they have different monthly options, with the highest being $150/month. Once you pay for it for 12 months, they will send you a check for $1663. There are also similar options that have higher limits, such as CreditStrong.com. Remember, it's always better to have higher credit lines. The higher the amount, the better. If you get credit lines with low limits, lenders will only want to give you low limits. There are many other companies like this that will give you additional credit if you have little to no credit history. The Great American Credit Secret course provides a full list of all the companies.

Notes

Notes

Notes

Notes

Notes

Notes

Notes

Notes

Notes

Notes

Notes

Notes

CHAPTER 3

Dying with an 800 Credit Score

Admittedly, the title of this chapter seems a little dismal. However, I really wanted to get the message across because we've seen this circumstance happen over and over again.

In this book, we talk a lot about people with bad credit, fair credit or no credit. But how about the people who have great credit? How about those who have excellent credit? I specifically wanted to make a chapter for them because often, those with great credit scores are not getting the maximum benefit or using that credit wisely.

My example is an elderly woman with a credit score of more than 800. This particular person had a dog that she nurtured and cared for. This dog was her only companion when her kids grew up and moved out of the house. She had a monthly stipend that she would be able to spend based on her retirement and Social Security and savings. She had a good life. However, the day came when her dog got very sick. Sad and afraid, she decided to take her dog to the hospital. When they got to the hospital, the veterinarian said, "I'm sorry, your dog could have a lot of life left in him. But with this rare condition that he has, there's only one treatment for it, and the procedure costs well over $6,000."

The old lady repeated to the veterinarian, "I don't have $6,000 to spend, but I don't want to lose my dog. Are there any other options?"

The veterinarian smiled and said, "Yes, we have alternative financing. All you will have to do is make sure you have decent credit, and we can get you financed to make monthly payments, and you can still save your dog's life."

The lady pondered this for a moment and asked, "So I will have to use my credit score?"

The veterinarian replied, "Yes." And added, "The procedure would surely save your dog's life."

The old lady pondered a second further and said, "I have over an 800 credit score, so I know my credit is not the issue." She said it very proudly. "But then I'm going to have something else on my credit report, and it will be additional debt." She continued, "They're also going to do a hard inquiry on my credit report, which hurts my credit."

Sadly, she opted not to save her dog. This is a sad but extreme circumstance as the dog went on and passed away.

What is even sadder is that there are many people with an 800 credit score in the same circumstance that do not know that they have the option to save their pet. They don't know that there is alternative financing for veterinarians and that you only have to make a small payment of maybe $140 a month, and little Pookie can live. But this comes with the ignorance of not knowing about credit. Still, like the elderly woman, some are paralyzed with fear. This fear comes from not knowing about credit. We fear what we don't understand.

Credit has always been a taboo subject if you really think about it. It's very hush-hush. You're not supposed to talk about your credit. When I was growing up, in my community, credit was something that was never discussed. There were many misconceptions and ill rumors in many households. Some of those rumors were and continue to be that credit is a trap and only use it in cases of extreme emergencies, or only use credit for an item that you have the same amount of money in the bank to fund.

Never use credit for something you don't have the cash to buy. That's a very popular expression many people use. It sounds good in theory, but it's entirely false.

Here in America, we have to play the credit game. If we have a job, and we can afford to pay whatever bill it is monthly to report to our credit report, I encourage you to do it. That is truly the only way that we are going to build up our credit over time.

The sad part about credit is that a lot of people have bad credit, not because they don't have the money to afford whatever they want, but because they don't know the power of it and therefore don't practice the discipline in earning it.

I've seen many millionaires, actors, lawyers, judges, and doctors with bad credit. In fact, the people in the highest income category are often the people that will have bad credit solely because they rely on the dollar.

What I would like to describe and break down for you are some of the things that you can have and afford with credit so that there is no guesswork as far as what credit can be utilized for. We've just discussed that you can use credit in veterinary situations. There are some banks that fund paying for a veterinarian. One of the most popular banks is called Care Credit.

That's what most of the population is familiar with, but there are many more.

Care Credit pulls from your TransUnion credit file to determine your creditworthiness and can be used by many veterinarians to save your animal. Care Credit can also be used for dental work. There's a company called Western Dental that's very popular in the United States that takes Care Credit. Essentially, Care Credit is a credit card for medical and dental purposes. For those seeking to get plastic surgery or cosmetic surgery, there are some medical offices that utilize Care Credit to finance you for those procedures as well.

It's important that you also know and understand that Care Credit is not the only lender out there for these types of procedures. There's also United Medical Credit and Lightstream that will finance you for medical expenses and cosmetic surgery. But there are many more alternatives even to those. We teach step by step directions on how to go about this in The Great American Credit Secret mentoring course.

I've seen people in awe of those who are traveling the world. They have great credit scores, and they've always wanted to travel the world. However, they have a theory in their brain that is incorrect. Those theories are that traveling costs massive amounts of money. Another theory or belief is that they cannot afford it. Another theory about credit is that it's bad to have multiple credit cards. All of these theories are, in fact, false. You want to have as many credit cards as you possibly can. A good credit profile has 21 tradelines on it, and those could be a combination of student loans, credit cards, a mortgage or an auto loan.

If that same person with the 800 credit score goes and gets approved for a few credit cards and stops using their debit card and instead uses that credit card, by the end of a year, they will be able to afford a free vacation, to a place like the Philippines, just on their points alone. An average flight to the Philippines is about $800 round trip. And since it's considered a third-world country, the prices are very inexpensive.

Let's continue with the Philippines example. I mentioned the $800 flight. How about a one-hour back massage? That will cost you about $6. The food in the Philippines is delicious and cheap. The cost of a luxury hotel in the Philippines is about $90 a night. In the United States, the same hotel or something equivalent would be $500 or $600 per night. Can you imagine going to that hotel and using your credit card for it? You're just earning points on top of points. That's the philosophy of those who understand *The Great American Credit Secret.*

These are the things people who truly understand credit start to realize. By just making everyday purchases, you can build and earn points. You can use your credit to leverage to get all kinds of things for free or at discounted prices. Some people have all these great dreams and never realize those dreams because fear paralyzes them from getting out there and living their best lives. Fear can be healthy when it comes to being responsible with your credit report, but it is debilitating when it stops you from achieving your lifelong dreams.

The best way to counteract this is to become aware of exactly what you want and how you can get it. Earlier, we discussed entrepreneurship. Someone with an 800 credit score may have dreams of starting their own business. Perhaps they have some hobby that they really like. They just don't know where they're going to get the money. They're afraid to use their

800 credit score because they've always heard that having multiple credit cards is a bad thing or that using their credit is not a wise move when this is exactly what they can utilize to fund the business of their choice. In fact, in many instances, if you have a great credit score and start a new company, you can go right away and get a business credit card. Sometimes, credit companies are very generous with the limits they give you. With business credit cards, the limits are generally much higher than for a W-2 or 9-to-5 employee.

It's sad that in today's society, most people who have an 800 credit score don't know how to utilize or leverage it effectively. I've heard many stories of people bragging they have an 800 credit score. That's great. The question then becomes, "What are you doing with the 800 credit score?" Are you living your lifelong dreams, or are you sitting on it, proud yet ignorant, not knowing how to utilize it except for bragging rights? I'm more impressed by someone who has a 710 credit score but is traveling the world using their points. The cold, hard truth is that many people who have a score in the 660-760 range live the most amazing lives because they're leveraging their credit; they use their credit cards regularly and pay them off. They fly around the world. They sometimes have multiple properties because they're getting Airbnbs and exotic cars and making money from creating income streams.

Some people are fascinated with the idea of having an 800 credit score but not fascinated with the idea of living their greatest life. How ironic.

Ultimately, the question becomes, which category do you want to be in?

Notes

Notes

Notes

Notes

Notes

Notes

Notes

Notes

Notes

Notes

Notes

Notes

Notes

CHAPTER 4

Debt, the Good, the Bad, and the Ugly

Debt is most often referred to in a negative light. Debt negotiation, debt settlement, and debt management are common ways of circumventing debt. However, it's imperative for you to realize that there are good forms of debt. For the vast majority of business owners, debt is necessary to propel and launch the business they truly desire. More often than not, consolidating or negotiating down debt is a bad practice.

This chapter is dedicated to explaining debt in its entirety, including how to structure it to work on your behalf in association with credit.

So the myth, the belief that debt in itself is bad, is incorrect. Why, you ask? This is mainly due to the fact that debt is a necessary component in the American credit system for getting things that we want and things that we need.

Often, when businesses are trying to get funding, if you don't have a multimillionaire uncle or parents, you may need to take out a loan to generate working capital to put into your company. Ask yourself, *Where would I be able to get the money or the funding if I couldn't take out a business loan or a personal loan or even utilize a credit card?*

Let's look at some specific examples. Take Donald Trump, for instance. Whether you love him or hate him is really not the point here. We need to focus on his past circumstances. Donald Trump is an individual who has gone into debt multiple, multiple times. It's common knowledge that he has filed for bankruptcy multiple times. Yet, if you look at Donald Trump, he's one of the richest people in the world. He's a billionaire. On top of that, he became President of the United States of America. How ironic.

Speaking of the United States, look at the country itself. The United States is trillions of dollars in debt and has been for years. A quick Google search shows our federal budget will run a deficit of more than $1 trillion this year alone, and currently, our national debt exceeds $23 trillion. Worse yet, our deficits and debt are projected to increase year after year. As far as the eye can see, America's fiscal outlook is the definition of unsustainable. Again, a Google search tells us about our national debt. However, Google also tells us (and so does every other reputable news media outlet out there) that if you list the most powerful countries in the world, the world's number one most powerful country is the United States. It has been since almost the beginning of time. The United States of America is considered the world's most dominant economic and military power. Economic, meaning that our economy is booming despite being trillions of dollars in debt. Are you starting to see a pattern?

If these examples show us that there are individuals, institutions, and entire governments thriving and flourishing despite being deeply in debt, what does this tell us? Debt in itself is not bad. It's how you utilize it that makes all the difference. Are you going into debt because you have a brilliant idea or invention to fund or because you want to take the girl of your dreams on a shopping spree?

Let's look at some examples of good debt, bad debt, and horrible debt.

Good debt, for example, would be someone developing a product for a company that many American consumers need, and you need a little bit of funding to bring the product to market. Therefore, you utilize the funds (your debt) to invest in a company, marketing, and advertising. You also invest in making your product for pennies on the dollar. Next, you're selling your product to many millions of individuals and making a very formidable return on your investment.

That's an example of good debt.

Another example of good debt would be owning a home. You need a place to live so that in itself is one reason to buy a home. Next, there's the principle of equity. Most homes in the United States are appreciating assets. The house is only going to go up in value. So all of the money you're putting into your home is like a savings account. That money will eventually go back to you. Many people who have lived in their homes for ten-plus years have hundreds of thousands of dollars in equity.

Another fact to remember is that you are essentially paying someone else's mortgage if you live in an apartment or are paying rent. Let's do some simple math: You pay rent for two years at $2,000 per month; that's a total of $48,000. You will never see that money again. However, let's say you own a house that costs $240,000. If you had paid that same $2,000 a month on your mortgage, you would have paid 20% of your house off. The equity left in your house would be more than that because, as we previously mentioned, equity generally increases year after year.

Let's take a different look at debt—a vehicle, for example. Many people know that for most of history, a car depreciates as soon as you drive it off the lot. However, there are people now that are renting the cars they own. There is an application called Turo where you can list your car to rent. Let's say you have two or three cars that you don't drive. You might have had them given to you or handed down from a cousin. You might even be paying $400 a month for one of the cars. But if you list that same car on Turo and it rents consistently, it would easily cover your $400 payment and likely put some extra cash in your pocket each month.

There are people taking it a step further. They rent out exotic cars. Sure, they may pay a heavy exotic car note, upwards of $1,500 per month, but only one or two rentals cover those costs. These are examples of good debt.

This is not to minimize bad debt. There are several forms of bad debt out there, and your job is to be aware of them and avoid them at all costs. Driving a fancy, expensive car when you do not live in a home and are not leveraging that car payment is a form of bad debt. Why is this? Because the car serves no purpose other than to impress people. But the reaction you are getting from people who see you in a nice car is not putting any money in your bank account. That's a form of bad debt. That's horrible debt (or ugly debt), especially because once the car is finally paid off, the value is usually far less than when you first got it.

Remember, the *outcome* should be *income.*

Another form of bad debt is procuring or getting a loan when you don't need it. Surprisingly, many people do this. They see that they're eligible to qualify for a loan, and they get the loan to pay off bills and things of that nature without a plan on how to pay it back. But that in itself is not a good practice. That will put you further into debt. So those are forms of bad debt.

Think about this. What would happen if there was no debt? If there was no debt, then we could not get a loan. When we go to a car dealership, we would be forced to buy the car outright. The biggest reason that debt is a good thing in the United States is that it directly correlates with your credit score. With credit, if you don't have any debt to show responsible payments on, then you will never build credit. Make no mistake, the smart utilization of credit is *The Great American Credit Secret.*

75% of our purchases in the United States are based on credit. But the only way that you can build credit is to go into some type of debt. Credit rules our country, and our country essentially rules the world.

Does that mean that credit or debt is a bad thing? No. You just have to learn to play the game in this country, especially now that you know that credit is the secret to leveraging your lifelong dreams. Your job is to play the game as smart as you possibly can. And that is exactly what this book is about.

We're giving you the principles and philosophies of utilizing credit and debt the smart way. So when you accumulate debt that reports to your credit, like a house or car, many make the mistake of paying that debt off as soon as they get the money to do it. This is not a smart idea because banks want to see a prolonged history of payments. So in the previous example, when someone has just purchased a car, and now they come into a lump sum of money, instead of paying it off, there are several other techniques you can use.

One technique is to set up autopay by putting money in an account and setting the car payment to draw automatically every month.

Another strategy is to double the payments because if there's a three-year history on the card and a three-year term on the car, you can cut that in half by making double payments every month. That's a quick strategy to build credit fast while still having enough time shown on your credit report. Eighteen months is sufficient for the banks to say, "Wow, this individual was on time for a prolonged period." The banks will not consider anything under three months a strong form of credit.

The tradeline that we previously discussed needs to have at least six months or more on the credit report for banks to take it seriously. Normally the length of time you should pay on an item is at least 6 to 24 months. *That's the secret...* Continuous payments over a length of time.

Remember, anything on your credit report stays on your report an average of seven years, and in a few cases, a positive tradeline will stay on longer. That's a good thing.

So next time you are looking at buying something or taking out a loan that will put you in debt, think about this question. Is this good debt? Is this bad debt? Or is this ugly debt?

Notes

Notes

Notes

Notes

Notes

Notes

Notes

Notes

Notes

Notes

Notes

Notes

Notes

CHAPTER 5

Secrets to Leverage Credit through Economic woes

The world has endured many national and global pandemics. Let's take a look back at some of the circumstances that have befell this nation: There is the AIDS epidemic, Ebola, Y2K, and the latest, the Coronavirus, Covid-19. National and global pandemics specifically impact the economy in multiple ways. The stock market, the housing market, car dealerships, and even banks change their methods and methodology when there is an economic crisis.

Why is this information important? Why does this matter? And more importantly, how can you survive a crisis economically?

Banks, for example, change a lot of their methods during a crisis. There's one particular bank called Pentagon Federal, also known as PenFed. PenFed is a great bank known for giving great auto rates and high-limit credit cards. They have one of the easiest methods to get signature loans. Before Covid-19, they were giving away signature loans for $25,000. That changed when Coronavirus hit. They changed their maximum loan to $20,000. When Covid-19 began to subside, PenFed jumped back in and raised their loan amount to $35,000 and a few months later to $50,000. This specific example shows that banks and credit unions can also be pandemic sensitive. Although there are other factors like inside bank health and market trends, the decision to increase or decrease loan amount is hugely impacted by the existence of a pandemic.

Those that know and understand *The Great American Credit Secret* can see the opportunity in potential economic disaster. I want to make it clear that I am not promoting financial gain at the expense of someone else's calamity. That is not the point. The point is for you to educate yourself so you can benefit from whatever is happening, good or bad, with the economy.

In times of economic disaster, some people become poor while others become rich. The difference between the two is simply a state of mind. It's a thought process. *That's the secret.*

When there's some type of economic disaster, the number one feeling is fear. People are paralyzed by fear. People make rash decisions based on that fear. People spend money based on fear. People hoard money based on fear. Use this information to form your own situations and outcomes.

For example, Billionaire Warren Buffett says that when the stock market crashes, everyone is selling their stock. Buffett contends that *that's* the time he starts to buy stock when they're at their lowest price. He's famously quoted, "The most common cause of low prices is pessimism—sometimes pervasive, sometimes specific to a company or industry. We want to do business in such an environment, not because we like pessimism (fear) but because we like the prices it produces." There's an example of someone who is not paralyzed by fear but instead saw an opportunity, and as a result, he's one of the richest men in the world.

Take the housing market, for example. There have been several housing market crashes throughout history. These are the times when many people go in and purchase those foreclosed homes and purchase those properties. They do fix and flips, or they sit on them and just let them gain their value back or rent them out. But to do so, you have to be in a position to do so, and you have to be ready. Even if you have light credit, meaning that you only have a few things on your credit, but you've been taking care of your credit, you can be in a position to take advantage of one of these foreclosed homes. Some of these homes are surprisingly inexpensive. I've seen homes sold for $20,000 and $30,000, which later are sold for ten times that amount.

Even car dealerships change their ways. For example, right now, cars are worth a lot more than they're normally worth. Typically, when you buy a car and drive it off the lot, it loses value. Most people know that, but currently, it's not one of those times. Cars are worth more now than ever before. It's likely that the car that you've purchased, if you purchased it within the last couple of years, has a higher value than it did when you bought it.

War is another economic crisis that affects the car market. Normally, gas prices skyrocket during wartime, so if you're going into the exotic cars business, you probably don't want to buy and rent out an SUV or a sprinter van when gas prices are really high. This is all information that you can utilize when making your moves.

Other important aspects to focus on during an economic crisis are products and inventions. When Y2K came out in 1999, everyone was fearful that the computers would crash. Many believed the computers would explode because the time clocks only went to 1999. Those who were keen and intelligent developed software that you could download to your computer, and the software only had one main function—to reset the clock to go to 2000 instead of 1999. They called this the Y2K relief kit. They sold everywhere, and they made millions because people were fearful that their computers would explode. This is a brilliant idea, and they sold it for $40-$50 when it probably cost less than a dollar to manufacture.

When the Coronavirus pandemic first hit, there was a huge demand for masks and gloves. There's a website called Alibaba.com. You can go on Alibaba.com and buy wholesale items in bulk for pennies on the dollar, literally pennies on the dollar. There were masks on there selling for as little as 5 cents each. And since it was a pandemic and people were fearful, those 5-cent masks were being resold for $2 and $3 each, along with gloves and hand sanitizer. People who had the foresight to buy low and sell at a profit made a fortune. They were taking advantage of an economic crisis.

So how does this relate to your credit? If you had a business credit card with a $40,000 limit or a personal credit card with $20,000, you would've been able to invest in 100,000 masks and 100,000 pairs of gloves. If you sold them for $3 apiece, that's $300,000 on your $5,000 to $10,000 investment.

You see, fear is a powerful emotion. People make buying decisions based on fear, and the truth is sometimes the fear is unwarranted, and sometimes it is a healthy fear that makes total sense. When the Coronavirus hit, people were rushing to department stores and grocery stores to buy all the tissue and toilet paper. There was a fear that they would run out of toilet paper. So, all the manufacturers, what did they start doing? They started boosting the cost of toilet paper.

Those that understand *The Great American Credit Secret* know when there's fear, *that* is the time to stop and think. That is the time to sit down and decide how you're going to proceed. Some of the best decisions are made at fearful times. Is this a time for you to save? Is this a time for you to invest? Is this an opportunity for you to contribute something to society that will help millions of people?

One thing for sure is that if you have bad credit or you don't have credit cards because you haven't understood the value, the philosophy, and the strength of having a strong credit profile, then you won't be in a position to act, even if you have a great idea.

You see, those who understand *The Great American Credit Secret* are ready for these types of catastrophic events to occur. In fact, they've put themselves in a position and aligned themselves to be ready for almost anything.

Author and evangelical educator Charles Swindoll perfectly captured this message in his famous quote, "Life is 10% what happens to you and 90% how you handle it." If you have your credit structured the right way, you'll be more prepared to handle and benefit from an economic crisis.

Notes

Notes

Notes

Notes

Notes

Notes

Notes

Notes

Notes

Notes

Notes

Notes

CHAPTER 6

Fact versus Fiction

When it comes to credit, there are a lot of myths and beliefs that are far from the truth. It seems everyone thinks they know exactly how credit works. Everyone has an opinion on what should and should not be done with credit. The truth of the matter is that many of the things that people believe about credit are not true. In this chapter, I will list some of those myths and explain why they are not necessarily true.

Myth 1: Do Not Get a Lot of Credit Cards

This is false for many reasons. One of the algorithms in a strong credit score is the number of accounts. So 21 tradelines or lines of credit, as we discussed, is considered excellent credit. Someone with 21 positive tradelines is far more attractive to the bank or to a lender than someone with two or three positive accounts or positive tradelines. The second reason is credit is just that—credit.

So if you have a $6,000 credit card, a $10,000 credit card, and a $15,000 credit card that's paid down to zero, that means you have $31,000 in available credit. The extra credit that's being unused is what increases your credit score—the more available credit, the better. So let's say someone else has only one, but they have a $20,000 limit. They may be inclined to think, *Hey, I have a credit card that has a limit bigger than all of yours. So maybe my credit is better.* Well, that's false. First, they have fewer tradelines and less total available credit on their credit profile. $31,000 is a bigger number than $20,000.

The next reason that it's good to have a lot of credit cards is because banks use something called "the mirror technique" in their algorithm. If they see you have multiple positive credit lines, they will normally "mirror" your highest credit line or even go higher. Banks also use other factors that depend on variables like your rent and income.

Another reason it's good to have a lot of credit cards is using a balance transfer. Many credit card companies offer a balance transfer option to transfer debt from one card to another or even open up a new card and transfer from that credit card to the newer credit card. These are examples that dispel the "too many credit cards are a bad thing" myth.

Now, having a lot of credit cards and going on a shopping spree with all of those credit cards with no means to pay them back, of course, is a recipe for disaster.

Myth 2: Real Estate Agents and Bank Tellers Know the Credit System

When it comes to credit, you'd think that many people in related industries such as banking and real estate would know everything about credit. This also is false. Bankers are just that—they are bankers. They are there to deal with banking, which is completely different from credit. The underwriting department in the bank is the only entity that truly understands how credit actually works. They're responsible for viewing the file and are trained to know what to look for on a credit report: What makes it strong, what makes it weak.

However, please do not assume that just because someone works at a bank or a car dealership, or a real estate agency that they know and understand the logistics of credit. Even so-called "credit repair agents" do not effectively know and understand credit. They may know how to dispute negative accounts and be familiar with piggybacking, but most credit repair agents do not know all of the ins-and-outs associated with credit. The sad truth is that most do not. So be vigilant when you're taking advice from someone in these positions.

Myth 3: Credit Karma Score Is Not Accurate

This is another common myth and is completely false. Why? Because there is no such thing as a real credit score. *There is no such thing as the right or a* ***real*** *credit score.*

This is because every institution has a different scoring model. What is a scoring model? A scoring model measures credit within that specific institution to see if a consumer is creditworthy to get approved for that item and, if so, for how much.

Do you recall in the previous chapter when I said banks use the mirror technique? Here's an example: When you go to a car dealership, many use something called Autoscore, but they have different scoring models that they use on top of that. Since it's a car dealership, what do you think they are looking at the most on your credit report? If you guessed a car, you are absolutely right. So someone with a 650 credit score who has successfully paid off four cars may have a higher credit score with a dealership than somebody who has a higher credit score who has never owned a car. *That's the secret.*

These are algorithms that individual lenders use when you're applying for a credit card. They use something called Bankcard, but they can also use any version of FICO UltraFICO, FICO 9, or FICO 10. It depends on that specific institution, and they use their inner algorithms to measure whatever your credit score is. Credit Karma uses something called Vantage. Wikipedia explains VantageScore as a consumer credit scoring model created through a joint venture of the three major credit bureaus. The model is managed and maintained by an independent company, VantageScore Solutions, LLC, that was formed in 2006 and is jointly owned by the three bureaus. Certain banks and institutions use VantageScore. So if you go to a bank or an institution that uses VantageScore, then chances are the score you see on Credit Karma will be very similar to what that banker institution has.

So there goes the theory that the score on Credit Karma is not real. The score on Credit Karma is just a VantageScore, and some institutions will use VantageScore.

Myth 4: Debt Is Bad

In our previous chapter, we discussed in detail why debt, in many ways, is good. Please review that chapter for insight.

Myth 5: Credit Takes a Long Time to Build

I remember as a child growing up, our parents didn't really understand a lot about credit, and one of the things they always told us was that good credit takes years and years to build. This instantly triggers a belief that we will not have good credit for many years. This is 100% false, and that is good news.

There are ways to build your credit quickly. You can go to a bank that has high-limit secured accounts and high-limit secured loans, and you can use your own money to secure those cards and loans. There's also, as previously discussed, Self Lender and Credit Strong. These installment accounts will put a tradeline on your credit report for $600 to $3,000 or even higher.

Suppose you do all of the above: You get one high-limit credit card utilizing your own funds. You get one secured loan using your own funds. You open up an account with Self Lender and Credit Strong and you let those build on your credit report for six months. Then you go and add an authorized user account that has, let's say, 15 years of history and $15,000. Chances are you will have around a 740 credit score (somewhere in that range), and you will have enough accounts with enough age to get approved for a small car loan or a decent-sized credit card. You can use this technique when you apply for credit cards, apply for five at a time, and you can instantly be approved for up to $100,000 in revolving credit! *That's the secret.* We discuss this in step by step detail in The Great American Credit Secret course.

So that means that someone with absolutely no credit, a blank credit profile, who has never used their credit can instantly build a strong credit score in six months. There goes that myth that credit takes a long time to build. However, keep in mind that the longer the age on the credit report, the better. If you have those same accounts and you pay on those for two years, instead of 6 months, will it be stronger? The answer is yes.

Myth 6: You will be approved for anything with a 800 credit score

False. Approvals have very little to do with your actual score. Instead, lenders and banks focus on what is in your actual file, and most lenders use the mirror technique. This means that if you are applying for a car they look primarily at your car history, or other installments. Lenders also look at your Debt to Income ratio and number of hard inquiries that you have previously had. Some lenders like Chase have a 5/24 rule, meaning that if you have applied for 5 credit cards in a 24 month period you will be automatically denied. Even with a 800 credit score. However there is one caveat: if the item you are applying for is secured like a house or car then the lender is more likely to approve you based on the score alone.

Myth 7: You Need to Get a Secured Card to Start Credit if You've Never Had Credit

This can be true and false. The truth is you *can* get a secured card to start credit. However, most secure cards have limits of $200 or $300 and are from subprime lenders. I recommend you stay far away from these. Someone with a $200 or $300 credit limit is not respectable in the eyes of the banks. This says that you are not accustomed to dealing with large amounts of money.

If you can only afford $200-$300, why would a bank finance you for an item of $5,000 or more? The answer is that they won't. A bank will not finance you for that amount or anything similar without some type of collateral or a large down payment. So instead of getting a small secured card to start your credit, get a large secured card or just foot the bill for a down payment on a vehicle. You can also open up those lines of credit as previously discussed with Credit Strong, but remember, getting a small secured card is a bad idea. The greatest method however, is to get a cheap car like a Prius. You can even rent it out because it is economical. I strongly recommend doing both.

I'm going to share with you a secret when it comes to funding and buying a vehicle. *Here's the secret.* If the item is something that a bank can take back from you, then it is easier to get. That means the parameters in your credit report do not need to be as perfect. If there's an unsecured item, the bank cannot take it back. Items that a bank *can* take back from you are secured loans and include houses and cars.

The ironic thing about this is that these are big items. They also make the biggest impact on your credit profile and give you the largest forms of buying power. But as I mentioned, they're the easiest thing to acquire because the banks can take them back. *That's the secret.*

Unsecured credit is more difficult to get because a bank cannot take it back. These include some loans, lines of credit and credit cards. If a bank gives you a $20,000 credit card, and you go and spend all of that money and do not pay them, a bank cannot come and take that credit card back. The funds which were on the card are already gone. The same applies for a loan or a line of credit. If a bank gives you a line of credit for $30,000 and you spend the $30,000 and do not pay the bank, the bank cannot come back and get their $30,000 back. The only means a bank has for recovery is to send you to collections or to try and sue you in court to recover their losses.

When it comes to acquiring those types of unsecured lines, a bank is going to look more strenuously at your credit report than someone financing an item that they can easily take back. In this book, I'm teaching you how to build your credit strategically so that you can get approved for those lines of credit. I want you to take advantage of securing both secured and unsecured loans. That's what this book is about. These are some of the things that the banks do not want you to know.

Notes

Notes

Notes

Notes

Notes

Notes

Notes

Notes

Notes

Notes

Notes

Notes

Notes

CHAPTER 7

Secrets of Utilizing Credit for Residual Profits

One of the techniques that I teach is utilizing credit to make a return on your investment with multiple streams of income and residual profits.

Have you heard the term "leverage your credit"? Making your credit work for you to receive passive income is a prime example of leveraging your credit. In this chapter, I'm going to discuss a few different ways and strategies in which you can do so.

A. Starting a Business

This is the age of entrepreneurship. Consumers are realizing they can start their own small company or business. Many have family and friends who have been successful, and they want to join the ranks of small business owners. However, few realize that one of the top reasons why businesses fail in their first two years is lack of income.

The question then becomes; how does one get funding? How do you gain funding if you don't have a rich uncle or rich parent who's going to loan you $50,000 or $100,000 for your entrepreneurial endeavors? A way to get funding is by building credit.

There are two different ways to do this with your credit: personal credit or business credit.

Let's go over a few details before starting a small business. A small business is any entity that makes under $5 million annually. In most cases, there will be no salary cap for a small business owner. As the founder, you can make as little or as much on the product or service that you generate.

So how do we build business credit? Let's start by talking about the business credit bureaus which monitor and report your score: Experian Small Business, Dun & Bradstreet, Equifax Small business, and SBFE (Small Business Financial Exchange). These are the bureaus that keep track of business credit scores, similar to how TransUnion, Equifax, and Experian keep track of personal credit scores. There are, however, a few differences.

First of all, personal credit scores range from 300 to 850. Business credit scores range from zero to 100. This is known as a Paydex score. A Paydex score measures the company's payment habits, similar to how FICO scores measure an individual's payment habits.

For example, an entity with a 0 to 49 Paydex score is considered high-risk. 50 to 79 is considered medium risk. And a company with an 80 to 100 score is the most favorable and considered low risk.

The second difference between personal and business credit is that in business, Dun & Bradstreet, which registers your payment experiences with vendors and suppliers, looks at what is known as trade references. It's imperative that you understand trade references are not credit card payments.

The third difference between business and personal is that in business, only transactions from the last two years are used in measuring your Paydex score.

There are other differences. When deciding whether to fund a particular company or business, some lenders may look at social presence such as websites, LinkedIn, or your Instagram page. They may also require that the business has a business address and a business phone number. If you're operating from your home, you can easily go online to obtain a virtual address to get an 800 number. There are companies you can contact, like Grasshopper, that will set you up with a phone number for $25 per month.

The course accompanying this book, *The Great American Credit Secret Master Mentoring Course*, shows you the specific steps to build out your Paydex score in as little as six months so you can get set up for funding. In the meantime, here are a few strategies to get funding for your new business by utilizing your credit.

The first thing is, do you have a company that's been in operation for two years? If not, then you can leverage your personal credit score as a personal guarantor, also known as a PG. Your profile should have paid installment loans. The more, the better because this is what gives you your buying power. If you have bad credit, you can consider contacting a credit consultation company such as Rapid Credit Boosters for a free consultation.

The next step to obtaining funding for your business is to have a website, business phone number, and business address. Again, do not use your home or a PO Box.

The next step is to set up a Duns number by contacting Dun & Bradstreet. Most lenders now pull from Experian business and there are multiple ways of building that as well. We teach step by step directions on that in The Great American Credit Secret Mentoring Course.

The last step is to contact the small business finance solutions provider that can strategically help you get funded. These companies include: Lendio, MagicBroker, Fund Box, and NAV. These are all viable options. You can also contact the SBA (Small Business Administration) to provide you with funding solutions. Again, if you watch the mentoring course available with this book, you will know the banks to go to get your funding, you will also learn step by step business secrets such as meeting the credibility check and other step by step strategies.

The second way to leverage your credit is by renting exotic cars on websites like Turo. As mentioned in a previous chapter, banks use the mirror technique when analyzing your credit report. If you have shown that you have paid off a vehicle on your credit report, this gives you car buying power. Car credit is different from personal credit in that whatever car you have paid off successfully, a bank will fund up to double that amount with little to no down payment.

So if you have paid off a $40,000 car loan, a bank will finance you for about an $80,000 vehicle from zero to 10% down. The caveat is that the rest of your credit is good. There cannot be recent missed payments or collections on your credit profile. There can't be a recent bankruptcy or any other derogatory factor.

Also, keep in mind that the car does not have to be completely paid off to be considered buying power. You can have a car on your credit report that you've paid on for two years and still owe 25% of the full value, and you will still get approved and funded if you meet the criteria. Keep in mind that when it comes to purchasing a vehicle outside of your credit, you need to have proof of income, and you also need to have a good DTI (debt to income ratio). Also keep in mind that the more the down payment, the better APR you will receive.

In this instance, if someone wants to go into the exotic car industry and use a car rental company to list those cars online for rent, keep in mind that you can go to several banks. The trick is to do it in a small window of time. Here are a couple of reasons why this is important.

If you go to the first dealership and get approved for a car, you might get one to five hard inquiries on your credit. You need to go to another car dealership as soon as possible. Banks will understand and be more forgiving of the multiple inquiries on your credit because you are looking for a car. They know that people go car shopping.

The second reason that a short window of time is important is that once you get approved for the first car, it reports to your credit in usually three to four weeks. Once it reports to your credit, your debt is raised significantly. It's now reported to your credit as a new vehicle and harms your debt to income ratio. So *the secret* is to go to dealerships within that small window of time before they report to your credit report. You can do this method over and over again.

Note: Please be responsible and make car payments for all of these cars—have a plan going into it.

I can tell you that exotic cars and even regular cars rent like hotcakes, especially in big cities. When you get this business rolling, it becomes a form of passive income because there's little work to be done as the cars are rented out daily.

The next method of utilizing your credit for residual income is authorized user tradelines. We've approached this subject several times in this book, but just to recap, an authorized user tradelines is when you add someone to your credit card and that credit history goes on *their* credit report. If you have a credit card with five years of payment history and a $5,000 credit limit, that is what will show up on the other person's credit report. *Here's the Secret.* The card needs to have a long history of on-time payments and a high credit limit, and it needs to be paid down under 10% utilization; meaning that if it's a $5,000 credit card, you want to have less than $500 on the card—the lower, the better.

This has become a very profitable business. Why is this? Because some people do not have any credit. Some people are unable to use any credit, so they don't know how to build credit. The only thing they know is to ask someone to add them to their credit card. A family or friend will do it for free, but they likely don't fully understand how this works. Companies legally have to offer authorized user tradelines to individuals. And if companies can do this, so can you.

If you have four credit cards with $20,000 limits, each credit card has five available slots to add users. Some credit card companies have more, like JPMorgan Chase and Barclays, and you can add people to those cards for a fee. An example, for a $20,000 credit card that has two years of payment history, a normal fee to add someone will be around $800 to $900. Multiply that by five because you get five slots, and then multiply that number by four different credit cards. These numbers add up quickly.

But when you're adding someone, you are really helping them. I've seen countless people get approved for homes and vehicles that would have otherwise had no chance had they not "piggybacked" on someone's authorized user tradelines. This is a great resource for you to gain ongoing, residual income and for someone else to benefit by jump-starting their credit.

As a reminder, there is a cap on the time someone can be added to an Authorized User tradeline; the normal industry standard time allotted is two months. You can add someone to your card for 60 days, allowing them enough time to get financed or funded for what they want, and then you can remove them from the card.

Important note: When adding someone to an Authorized User tradelines, there is no way that they can hurt your credit unless you give them a credit card, so do not give them a credit card. However, keep in mind that your actions can hurt them. If you miss a payment or you max out your credit card, that person's credit will fall. So if you're in the authorized user tradelines game, please remember to be responsible with those credit cards or put them away and do not use them. It's a good idea to look up your state laws because some states (like Georgia) have specific laws regarding credit.

The last form of utilizing your credit to create residual profits is Real Estate.

Typically, real estate experts say you have to have good credit. This is very true. The secret is that real estate works a little differently with credit. Why is this? With real estate, the only thing that matters when it comes to credit is the score and your debt to income ratio, and that's it. So with real estate, you can utilize your credit. You can do a fix and flip. You can buy foreclosed properties. You can get cheap properties. Texas has very affordable properties. You can get a property for a hundred thousand dollars, with a very small down payment and rent it on Airbnb.

One of the beautiful things that I love about real estate is that it's the one thing that almost always goes up in equity. It's the one asset that almost always appreciates. I have very rarely seen a situation in which it depreciates. Those that understand *The Great American Credit Secret* know there is tremendous power in owning a mortgage because it opens up countless doors. It gives you buying power, leverage, equity, credit, and stability. If you are not paying your own mortgage, you are paying someone else's.

Notes

Notes

Notes

Notes

Notes

Notes

Notes

Notes

Notes

Notes

Notes

Notes

Notes

CHAPTER 8

Secrets the Bureaus Don't Want You to Know

Once upon a time, there was a man who owned a neighborhood market. As the market grew bigger and bigger, the owner began to recognize and become familiar with his clients who shopped in the store. Often, when someone would not be able to purchase an item, they would ask him if it would be okay to pay him on their payday. It became known in the neighborhood that he would offer these terms to consumers he was familiar with. The owner kept a notebook that showed who owed, what day they would pay, and if they would pay on time. He used this notebook to determine whether or not he should continue extending credit to certain clients. He also used this notebook of information to set what limits to give to each customer.

Years later, when the man decided to sell the store, he handed the new owner the notebook. The new owner was thrilled because there was a system in place in which he could continue to sell products even when clients did not have the means to pay upfront.

The previous store owner left and started a company called American Retail Credit. His idea was this, since there is a huge market for collecting consumer spending habits, he would gather that information and sell it to lenders and stores so they could decide whether to extend credit to their clients based on his data. He developed a system in which he could track who was paying on time, who wasn't, and what limits they were able to pay. He formulated a whole system based on a consumer's spending behavior.

On one particular occasion, a lender contacted a woman saying that she did not pay on time, and therefore, they were trying to collect their money. That lady was the first person to ask, "Well, how did you get my information? How did you find me? How did you know that I had not paid? How do you know what amount it is?"

Although the lady was not completely sure, she felt that something was amiss. She truly felt like her rights were being violated. Although she did owe the debt, she contacted an attorney. The attorney came in and looked at the case and said, "You know what? You're absolutely right. How did they get your information? How did they contact you? How do they know your address and phone number? How do they know the actual amount? How does this company have so much of your personal information when you did not give it to them?"

The lady sued American Retail Credit, the company the liquor store owner had started and won millions of dollars in damages. This is a true story.

This lawsuit prompted the government to enact new laws, including the Fair Credit Reporting Act.

One of these clauses in the Fair Credit Reporting Act is that anything negative, false, or misleading on a credit report must be removed. Another is that lenders cannot pull your credit without your consent. Because of that lawsuit, these laws are in place now and are meant to protect the consumer.

The irony to this story? To stay in business after being shamed in court for conducting shady business practices, American Retail Credit reinvented itself and changed its name to... Equifax. Yes, the same Equifax that is known as today one of the three biggest credit bureaus.

This previous story illustrates several points about credit and the bureaus.

One of *The Great American Credit Secrets* is the perception that the bureaus are government entities. They make it sound this way for a reason. They're called bureaus, as if they are a branch of the government like the Federal Bureau of Investigation (FBI). The word *bureau* is used to trick consumers into thinking they're associated with the government—they are not. They are for-profit companies that constantly make mistakes. Credit bureaus exist to analyze your data and report items to your credit report. They exist to make money by working closely with lenders and collection agencies. Think about when you sign up for Experian.com or Equifax.com. They have a lot of these offers for credit cards and things of that nature. This is their way of making money.

Fortunately, the bureaus are now forced to uphold the Fair Credit Reporting Act. So, if there is an inaccurate item on your credit report, by law, they have to remove it.

Speaking of Equifax, in 2017, the company had a huge breach. Most people know and are familiar with this breach. Millions upon millions of consumers' data was exposed and Equifax was sued. Remember, this is the same company that got sued the first time but this time they were sued with a different, fancier name. Equifax, Transunion and Experian adopt the name "bureau" to make it seem as if it's a government agency similar to "bureau of investigations" or something of that nature. Do not be fooled. These are out for profit businesses that have started to make money. That's why if you go to their website they are offering you credit cards in which you may or may not get approved for. They get paid every time you sign up. It's all a business. Speaking of these card offers, please know that just because they offer them to you does not mean that you will qualify. Always be diligent about which credit card you want and never sign up for over the counter offers because it will "save you 20% off today". That's a permanent decision based on a temporary reward.

In regards to the credit bureaus the truth is that they walk a fine line with regard to consumer credit. The bureaus are made to sound like these powerful entities, but in reality, their power is limited. This is important for you to know. Many times, when there's a collection or something negative on their credit report, consumers say, "Hey, this was my item, therefore, I must pay it." Most people think that way and either pay what is shown they owe or work out a payment plan. Very few consumers question the validity of the item that's on their credit report.

For example, if you have an account with T-Mobile and you didn't pay your bill, it will show up on your credit report. Again, most people will eventually just pay whatever T-Mobile says they owe. However, the truth is that most of the time, there is some type of inaccuracy with the negative item on the credit report (i.e. interest or total amount owed). Some lenders see a collection account as an opportunity to inflate the account and add a little bit of extra interest on top of it. Then, when the debt is sold to the collection agencies, they, too, see this as an opportunity to add a little bit of extra interest to it.

What the bureaus do not want you to know is that they have to show an account of every single thing that is on your credit report and produce documentation of when you signed the document.

This is why I always recommend disputing whatever is on your credit report. It's not that you're saying the item is not yours, but you are forcing them to show you what the actual item is. *What was the actual amount of money that I spent? How much money do I actually owe you?*

The bureaus are fallible. Statistics show an average of 76% of credit reports with derogatory items have some type of mistake. 76%! According to the Fair Credit Reporting Act, if there's a mistake, it must come off your credit report. This is *the secret* the bureaus do not want you to know.

Another thing the bureaus don't want you to know is that they're bombarded daily with paperwork. They have paperwork coming in and going out for consumers. They also have to process paperwork and data for lenders and other companies. So when someone is writing them, dispute upon dispute, saying, "What is this item?" Often, the bureaus don't want to foot the bill for the staffing to research and dig and produce paperwork on that account that's only for a couple of hundred dollars. The negative items on your credit report may be older and about to fall off. Remember, negative items only stay on for seven years. In other cases, there will be collection accounts that are on your credit report that have already been paid. In theory, if there's no more money to be made off of an account, why would the bureaus or collection agencies continue to fight it? All of these items are easier to dispute if you take the time to do it.

Here's another thing the bureaus don't want you to know. They often put medical bills on your credit report to take advantage of what can be a confusing situation. Think about it. If you're being admitted to the hospital, it is likely for a serious ailment. You might be incapacitated or not able to fill out the insurance paperwork, so the hospital might not record your information. When you're discharged, if the hospital didn't get your medical insurance or your personal information and you never receive a bill, it is sent as delinquent to your credit report. This happens! Fortunately, it's an easily disputed item.

Here's something else the bureaus don't want you to know regarding medical collections. HIPAA law specifically states that anything that has your medical information is private. They cannot talk or share anything regarding your medical care. They cannot share your medical information with another collection agency—it's illegal. So if your medical treatment is bought by a collections agency, that's a violation of HIPAA law. This is how you can easily remove medical items from your credit report.

In fact, medical bills are so misleading and have been such a problem that by 2023, the government has proposed a law that would restrict medical bills from being reported.

In the meantime, just know the facts about credit bureaus; they're out for profit, fallible companies that make a lot of mistakes. Whenever something goes on your credit report, do not just assume it is accurate because one derogatory item can cause you to pay a higher interest rate over the next year, five years, or seven years until it falls off.

Even if you pay for the item that's in collection, most of the time, it does not come off your credit report. The only way it will come off your credit report is if the lender sends you a "pay for delete" letter stating that once you pay the item, they will delete it from your credit profile.

Be vigilant when you're talking on the phone to a lender and trying to determine how to pay an account that they do not say misleading statements such as, "Yeah, we will report it as paid." Or, "Yes, we will show that this item is not harming you anymore." These are misleading because although the item is paid, it still haunts you. Remember, when banks look at your credit report, they also look at closed accounts. *That's a secret.* It does not matter if the negative item was five years ago, the account is closed, and it's paid off. Lenders still look at it. That's still a negative account, and the banks see it. The banks know the history of a client. This is another one of America's Great Credit Secrets.

Notes

Notes

Notes

Notes

Notes

Notes

Notes

Notes

Notes

Notes

Notes

Notes

CHAPTER 9

Secrets About Credit Repair Companies

Now more than ever, people are starting to realize that if there are inaccuracies on their credit reports, things can be done. In the past, when a lender called and threatened to put something on a consumer's credit report, many individuals just paid whatever they were told to pay. Others were knowledgeable enough to set up a payment plan. However, few knew that the charges could and should be disputed.

When a lender sells a debt to a third-party company, they can apply their own interest on top of the original debt. This is an example of something that should not be on your credit report, and there are many others. In this chapter, I'm going to examine credit repair and credit repair companies. *What do they do? Is it legal? What are the legalities of it and how do I choose the correct one if that is the route that I'm going to go?*

First of all, I cannot emphasize enough the importance of fixing your credit. If there is an inaccurate item on it, it has to come off by all means or you will be suffering by paying more for everything! I repeat, if there is something negative on your credit report, even one item, you're going to pay more for everything. You're going to pay more interest for everything. So find a way to get rid of it.

The truth about credit repair is that you can absolutely do it yourself. Here are some of the ways.

If you have something negative on your credit report and you don't know where it came from, that could be identity theft. If you believe you have been a victim of identity theft, there is an easy way to dispute that on your credit report. Let's say someone opened up three or four accounts using your credit profile. They somehow got a hold of your information, your Social Security number, birthday, all of this pertinent information, and opened up accounts. What you can do is call a non-emergency police line and file a police report. When you file the police report, what you are saying is, *I do not know these things on my credit report. I did not do them. I do not know who did. I have been a victim of identity theft.*

It normally takes about two weeks to receive a police report, and you can send that information to all three credit bureaus. This is the fastest way to get rid of negative items on your credit report—the number one fastest way.

The next way that you can get rid of negative items on your credit report is to pick up the phone and call the bureaus directly. This does not work every time, but sometimes it does. You call the bureaus, tell them about the suspicious item on the credit report, you verify who you are and you tell them that this is not your item. It doesn't happen often, but occasionally, they will take the item off your report and out of their system right there on the spot.

Sometimes the bureaus will ask you to bring in or submit paperwork, and this brings me to my next point. When it comes to credit repair, you can fix your credit yourself. You can do it yourself by going online and reading and researching. YouTube has videos about every single credit repair tip known to man, including disputing items with the FTC (Federal Trade Commission) and CFPB (Consumer Finance Protection Bureau). The one concern with this is that different people have different methods, so it's hard to decide which is the right one for you. But the point is, you *can* do it yourself. Just like you can learn to fix a car, shampoo your carpet or groom your dog, you have the choice to learn how to fix your credit or hire a credit repair company to do it for you.

If you do decide to fix the items yourself, there are certain letters that you can use. There's something called a 609 letter. The 609 letter shows how you can dispute whatever items are on your credit report. The process is fairly simple. You fill out the 609 letter with all of your information: name, Social Security number, and address. You need to include a color copy of your ID, Social Security card, and a copy of a recent utility bill. Mail that letter to all three of the credit bureaus explaining the inaccuracies you have found on your report.

Credit repair companies exist because many people do not have the time, energy, or knowledge to dispute their own files. Here are some things that you need to know about credit repair companies. There are good credit repair companies and bad credit repair companies. With credit repair, there are not a lot of licenses, professional certificates, or degrees that need to be obtained to run these companies. So when you look at a credit repair company, the number one thing you should look for is credibility.

Who are the owners? How do they operate? What type of credentials do they have that will substantiate them to be an owner of a credit repair company? What are the reviews online? Do they offer any type of money-back guarantee if you are unsatisfied? Do they offer a written agreement? Do they offer a contract?

Be wary of credit repair companies that only offer a very small payment method. Typically, these companies take a very long time to dispute your credit repair. Sometimes they only dispute one item at a time, one bureau at a time, meaning that whatever small monthly payments you are making, you will be making for two to three years before your credit is finally repaired. In two to three years, a lot can happen. I do not recommend these types of companies.

One of the most reputable credit repair companies is called Rapid Credit Boosters. You will receive a written agreement, and they have an outstanding reputation for boosting credit quickly. Many of these credit repair companies offer authorized user tradelines, also known as Piggybacking. We have talked about this several times throughout this book. In Piggybacking as an authorized user, you are added to someone else's credit card for the purpose of "piggybacking" on the benefits of their high-limit, low utilization card to boost your own credit score.

Credit repair companies also offer these types of products to help boost credit scores. In choosing the credit repair company, ask them upfront which methods they use to secure your data. A good credit repair company has encryption, and or they have their representatives sign a non-disclosure or confidentiality agreement. That way, you know that your information is protected. If their answers are not sufficient or you get a bad feeling about them, do not hesitate to choose a different company. If there is no type of written agreement, do not sign up with that company. *This is very important.* It is illegal for a credit repair company to offer a specific timeframe for your credit to be repaired. So, if there's a credit repair company guaranteeing your credit will be fixed in 30 days or any specific amount of time, you know that the company is not following credit laws.

If there is a credit agency you feel is doing something illegal, you can report them to the Better Business Bureau and several other entities.

Most credit repair companies listed on Google know that they are dealing with pertinent information, and they know how important it is to do the credit repair process correctly and efficiently.

Notes

Notes

Notes

Notes

Notes

Notes

Notes

Notes

Notes

Notes

Notes

Notes

CHAPTER 10

Debt Consolidation Secrets

It's essential that you understand the difference between debt consolidation and credit repair. Although they are closely associated, they are not the same. You have to know how they work with each other in order to achieve your ultimate goals.

Let me explain. Debt consolidation is when you have an overwhelming amount of debt, and you want to find a way to pay it down by consolidating, which means bringing it together. Consolidating debt is not the only way to get rid of debt. And that's what this chapter is about.

One of the algorithms of credit involves your debt. How much debt is owed, for example. So if someone has a credit card for $10,000 where $9,000 is spent, that's $9,000 in debt. Does that necessarily mean they have bad credit? No, it doesn't. It just means that there is a high amount of debt.

That is, however, important because sometimes, when you are trying to get financed for an item, the fact that the debt is there, and it is outstanding, will hurt your chances. One, because debt lowers your credit score. The second reason is that debt hurts your debt to income ratio.

Let's talk about some of the pros and cons of debt and debt consolidation. We've talked about how debt hurts your credit score. It brings your credit score down, especially if you have a maxed-out credit card or a couple of auto loans. Debt will also hurt your debt to income ratio. If you're trying to get approved for a high-ticket item, the lenders can say you don't qualify because you have too much debt.

One of the benefits of debt is that it can help build good credit. You have to start with debt to build good credit. We spoke in earlier chapters that debt is a necessary component of maintaining credit. I do not agree with the philosophies of Dave Ramsey and Suze Orman, who speak against having debt, because I think debt is necessary for us to be able to build a strong credit profile. Keep in mind that building a strong *personal* credit profile is how we're often able to start building our *business* credit profile.

Another pro of debt, which is growing in popularity, is utilizing it to make residual income. We spoke about some of the methods and techniques in the previous chapter, leveraging credit to make residual income.

Now let's talk about the good and bad of debt consolidation. I'll start with the bad. Some institutions offer debt consolidation for overwhelming credit card debt. The company contacts you and offers to consolidate all of your debt for this one amount. In many cases, their strategy is to instruct you to stop paying on your credit cards for three to four months. After that time passes, the company contacts those individual lenders to make a deal where they're essentially saying, "Hey, Jane Doe is not paying these bills. So, would you be willing to accept this amount of money?" They add their own fees on top of the negotiated settlement, and then you start making payments to the consolidation company for a lot less than what you would have originally paid.

Does this method work? Yes, and no. Yes, it works because you can pay a lot less money than you would have had to originally pay on those bills, but at what cost? The problem is that once you stop paying your bills, your credit report takes a hit. You're going to have missed payments on your credit report. And when you go and try to get high-limit credit cards or other credit cards, you will get turned down or only get approved for subprime credit cards with high interest rates and low limits. Is that worth it just so you can save some money? No.

The reason why it is not worth it is that there are better techniques of consolidating your debt. Be wary of this particular type of debt consolidation. I strongly advise against it.

Another form of debt consolidation is a debt consolidation loan. Sometimes debt consolidation loans can be very helpful because they have great terms and a low interest rate. If this is your particular situation, and you have outstanding debt, let's say $40,000 worth of credit card debt, and this institution may offer you a $40,000 loan with small monthly payments. This may be a great incentive for you, especially because your score will increase as those credit cards are being paid down. You get more points for revolving credit, meaning that your new installment loan will not override the loss in points that you will gain from your credit cards being paid down. The other benefit is that then you have an installment loan on your credit report that you're making monthly payments on. Your score will potentially increase while your debt is being reduced.

Again, it is better to have less revolving debt than less installment debt. This is because revolving debt targets your credit score in a different way than installment debt. Most people with installment loans are utilizing whatever the installment is. For example, if it's a car or if it's a house, you have to live in that house. You have to drive that car to work. So a bank does not look as unfavorably on installment loans.

A signature loan or a debt consolidation loan is a form of an installment. It's better to have a $40,000 installment debt consolidation loan and remove the $40,000 in debt from the personal credit cards. This method of debt consolidation is highly recommended. It also keeps your credit report in tip-top shape. In fact, it makes it stronger because the more you're paying your installment loan, the stronger your credit score is getting. And you have $40,000 revolving credit back open to utilize if you need it.

The next form of debt consolidation would be balance transfers. In many cases, people have high debt, but they still have good credit. Their debt is just a little bit high. So if you've been with an institution for a particular time, many times, you can open up another credit card with that institution and do a balance transfer of some portion or all of that debt to a new card; you can also do this method with different institutions. Remember, with revolving credit or credit cards, the higher the amount you owe, the higher the interest you have to pay every month. If you split that up from one card to the next, not only does the monthly bill go down, but the interest that you're paying also goes down.

In many cases, you can get a couple of balance transfer cards and repeat that process. If you are getting approved for a high-limit credit card with great terms, this is a phenomenal way to help reduce your debt.

Many times when you open up balance transfer cards, you will get a 0% interest rate for the first year. Many banks are starting to offer 0% interest for the first 18 months. Remember, banks are competing to earn your business because without you, they cannot stay in business—they're fighting for your business. When someone comes in with a good credit report or a decent credit history, they jump through hoops to get you approved for those balance transfer cards. This is another reason why I cannot emphasize enough the importance of having good credit.

There's another form of getting rid of debt when you are submitted to a credit repair company or when you are disputing your own credit yourself. For whatever reason you no longer have the vehicle and the bank is telling you that you owe $10,000. It's now on your credit report as a negative item because they say you missed the last four monthly payments. This is a common occurrence that happens in the industry because auto dealerships and banks have their own tools and mechanisms they can use for collecting debt on automobiles. The dealership then repossesses or takes the car back from you, and then auctions it off. They charge you a certain percentage of fees for all kinds of miscellaneous items (towing fee, dealer fee, hookup fee, late payment fee, auction fee, gas fee, and any other fee they can think of).

Next, you submit the derogatory item on your credit report to a credit repair company because it's now a negative item on your report and the credit repair company is eventually going to get it removed (an auto repossession on your credit report is an average of 80 to 110 points once removed). Let's say, however, that the credit repair agency disputes the car on the credit report. Remember, that they are not necessarily saying that the car does not belong to you, they're disputing any inaccuracies with that car. That car on your credit report shows $10,000 in debt. That $10,000 debt is going to affect you when you go to buy a house, buy a car, buy anything. They're going to still say that you owe $10,000 in arrears and that debt is going to count against you even though you no longer own the car.

Once that car gets removed from your credit report, your credit score goes up for multiple reasons. One, you have $10,000 worth of debt that is no longer on there. The second reason is obviously if there were negative items on your report, those are no longer on there either. The question that remains is, *what happens to the debt? What happens if they find an inaccuracy and remove the car from your credit profile?* Does this mean that you do not owe that $10,000 to the lender anymore? No, you still owe the dealership that $10,000. The only way you do not owe the dealership the $10,000 is if you have gone to court and won a lawsuit against them that shows that you don't owe the $10,000. But for the purpose of credit repair, you've achieved the success of not having that debt on your credit report. Congratulations.

After that auto is removed and someone pulls your credit report, they are not going to see that. All they're going to see is your good credit and that is a beautiful thing. But what happens with the $10,000 debt that the lender said you owe? Well, they put it in the files and they store it deep down in their "basement." Very rarely will they come back in and put it on your credit report. Why do most consumers pay off the auto in full, and let it sit on their credit report for 7 years? Because most people do not understand *The Great American Credit Secret*. They do not understand that they can fight that derogatory item on their credit report. Again, most people are led by fear. A lot of times, it's fear of the unknown and lack of knowledge. Consumers do not know their rights, and they do not know of laws like the Fair Credit Reporting Act which allow them to legally remove inaccuracies from their credit report. Auto dealerships focus on those types of individuals. They focus on consumers who just want to hurry up and make a payment so that they can stop the collection calls.

In this instance, once the car is removed from your credit report, you have a decision to make. You have options if you still owe money. Some people will just not pay the dealership since the car has been removed from their credit report. The thought is it should not have been there in the first place. There may be some consequences to this, but putting it back on your credit report is not one. They can still continue to call you and harass you, although normally, after a certain amount of time, they stop.

You can also contact the dealership, and you do not have to tell them that the item has been removed because it's none of their business, but you can say, "Hey, listen, you had a $10,000 item on my credit report. Why don't we set up payment arrangements? I will pay you $25 a month." This will stop the harassing phone calls and the car is no longer on your report. With this tactic, you have achieved the car not being on your credit report. $25 a month is not a lot, but most lenders will take it and you can move on.

Knowing *The Great American Credit Secret* is imperative. You have to protect your credit at all costs. That is your bread and butter. You want to be able to utilize and leverage your credit. It is my recommendation that everyone starts a business even if it does not have a specific function or you're not 100% sure of what it is that you want to do. Start it anyway. Start with a business name. It can be your first and last name. Once you have good credit, you can get a credit card under that business and have that credit card if you need it. There's no law that says you have to have a business that is booming and generating income to get approved for a business credit card.

Most millionaires and successful people have a few commonalities. One, they have multiple businesses. Two, they have multiple bank accounts. Three, they have multiple houses or homes. Most millionaires deal in multiplicity and abundance, so why not start thinking and acting like a millionaire? Leverage your credit. Leverage your personal credit. Build your business credit. *That's the secret.* It is not that difficult, and it could change your life.

Notes

Notes

Notes

Notes

Notes

Notes

Notes

Notes

Notes

Notes

Notes

Notes

Notes

CHAPTER 11

Scoring Models and What They Mean

A normal question in the credit world is, "Why is my score different?" There are two main reasons. First, your score may be different from bureau to bureau because they report things differently. They don't always report across the board.

For example, if you have a Capital One credit card, it is going to report to all three bureaus, TransUnion, Equifax, and Experian. However, if you have a collection show up on your credit report, it is not likely that it is going to report to all three bureaus. It might report to one or two, which means that those one or two bureaus will have a lower credit score than the third bureau.

Even though these are three entirely different companies, most things, when they report, hold the same numerical value. So the only reason that the score would be different in this instance is that something got reported to one that did not get reported to the others.

The second reason why your credit score may vary is because of something called a scoring model, there are tons of different models which we discussed earlier. If you are familiar with Credit Karma, Credit Karma uses something called Vantage. Another scoring model would be FICO or FICO 8 scoring models. These are models that measure algorithms differently depending on what the lender's needs are. For example, there's a scoring model called Autoscore within the auto industry. So Autoscore gives more points for paid-off autos and is normally used by car dealerships.

Let's look at a few different scoring models and see how they operate. Bankcard Score is used when someone is applying for a credit card. Many banks and institutions use this to look at and monitor your credit card banking.

Your mortgage score can also fluctuate. People look at Experian or Credit Karma when they go to get a mortgage and they come back and say, "Wow! My mortgage score was a lot lower (or higher) than what is on Experian. Why is it so different?" Well, it's different because in a mortgage score, they're looking at your mortgage history, they're looking at your installment history, then they look at everything else. So after the first two mortgage parameters, other factors can have varying importance depending on the company reporting.

When learning *The Great American Credit Secret,* it's important that you understand the difference between scoring models and how they work. Going back to our initial illustration of varying credit scores, you can use this to your advantage.

Here's an example: Let's say your TransUnion score is very high, but for some reason, on Equifax and Experian, your scores have dropped. When you go to get qualified for a car or any other loans, you can go to a bank that specifically pulls from TransUnion. These banks include

LifeStream and Navy Federal Credit Union. They only pull from TransUnion. *That's the Secret.* You can do individual Bureau pulls because most banks only pull from one institution. Conversely, in real estate, they're going to pull from all three institutions so be sure to do whatever credit repair that needs to be done before you apply for a mortgage.

You can call a bank and ask, "What Bureau do you pull from?" Some banks won't tell you where they pull from, and others will.

Notes

Notes

Notes

Notes

Notes

Notes

Notes

Notes

Notes

Notes

Notes

Notes

Conclusion

In the United States, money talks but credit holds the conversation. Don't be fooled, because ignoring your credit is financial self sabotage. Instead, gain a clear picture and understanding of what your goals and dreams are and then execute by building and leveraging your credit. In this book you have learned tricks, strategies and secrets to live the life of your dreams with credit. Now you have the ability to think outside of the box, and know that there are multiple ways to achieve your goals. There is the traditional way, and the non-traditional way, but the point is—THERE IS ALWAYS A WAY.

Disregard all of the rumors you've heard and learn to separate fact from fiction. I implore you to read this book over and over until you have developed a deep understanding of the undisputed truth—leveraging credit is the biggest secret on earth! Once you understand that concept and learn to master it, you will achieve all of your lifelong dreams. For more information about how to get started in your new credit repaired life go to: rapidcreditboosters.com.

THANK YOU FOR READING MY BOOK!

DOWNLOAD YOUR FREE GIFTS

Just to say thanks for buying and reading my book, I would like to give you a few free bonus gifts, no strings attached!

To Download Now, Visit:

I appreciate your interest in my book, and I value your feedback as it helps me improve future versions of this book. I would appreciate it if you could leave your invaluable review on Amazon.com with your feedback. Thank you!

Made in the USA
Monee, IL
12 November 2026

79e76511-6201-4762-9e2b-56657fa47b73R01